Why Chloe Loves Christmas

Written By Elle Kaye
Illustrated by Yuliana Bezrodnaya
Special thanks to Jacek Pawlowski for making Chloe's book look great!

....and rolling in the warm Summer sun...

….and romping in crunchy Autumn leaves…

But most of all Chloe loves...

CHLOE LOVES CHRISTMAS!

Why does Chloe love Christmas?

Is it because of beautiful Christmas carols to sing to?

Yes!

But that's not her favourite thing...

Yes!

But that's not her favourite thing...

Is it because of the happy snow family

she builds in the yard every year?

Is it because of the delicious cookies

she makes for Santa?

Is it because Santa leaves her presents in her stocking?

Then what is Chloe's favourite thing?

...and the fresh, piney smell.

ISBN: 978-1-9904280-3-6

Copyright © 2021 by Elle Kaye
All rights reserved. This book or any portion thereof
may not be reproduced or used in any manner whatsoever
without the express written permission of the publisher
except for the use of brief quotations in a book review.

www.ingramcontent.com/pod-product-compliance
Lightning Source LLC
Chambersburg PA
CBHW061350010526
44107CB00011B/886